Introduction.

I have studied and written about technology and nature for several years. I see them as two forces which have remarkable similarities in purpose and design, this is because mankind has replicated so many of nature's functions when we develop our machines. If you think about what we have achieved in terms of innovation we have to admit we are copycats more than inventors. Our technology has followed a parallel path of evolution. Nature created us and viruses, we then created computers and computer viruses. Earth has its natural disasters, and we have man made ones.

Nature in comparison with our technology has always had a superior production line, able to ensure a circular and self-sustaining system, whereas whatever we do has been linear, self-serving and independent of any greater scheme.

The chances of an extinction level event by a major natural disaster or catastrophe brought on by the human race are equally probable. When I started writing this feature I asked myself if this was a once in a life time opportunity. The answer I came up with was an insensitive statement, but true nonetheless: 'a pandemic is a career highlight for a *Future Thinker.*'

This will not be a once in a lifetime opportunity because the probability of a second wave of Covid-19 or another pandemic in my lifetime are high.

Scenario planning must be part of all business strategies as we take a step into the Future World. This manuscript offers insight on what we have learnt from Coronavirus, man's reactions to a natural disaster and how to prepare for more in the coming years.

We should have known.

Our leaders were warned about a virus like Covid-19. Disease experts have highlighted the accelerated outbreaks over decades. Since 1980 there have been more than 12000 that have infected and killed millions of people, to name a few: MERS, H1N1, Dengue, Ebola and Zika. Mother Nature has given us plenty of warning shots.

SARS was a bad pandemic, but when compared to Coronavirus it seemed to disappear overnight with little to no economic ramifications. In 2019, I referenced natural disasters in an article, and then again in early 2020, even before lock down had been mentioned, I wrote a brainstorming article on how I might quarantine during the worst case scenario of the outbreak.

Added with other obvious factors like increased international travel, populated cities and more interaction with animals, preparations for a pandemic was well overdue.

We know change is the only constant in the universe and adaptation is essential to survival. We are conscious beings and *change* comes only once we decide upon it. Unfortunately we don't always make decisions when needed, and once we have it is occasionally not the finest choice, resulting in a stumble, a fall, and landing of ourselves into a very unpleasant situation. Only then do we amend our habits, and in this extreme situation, change the very trajectory of our species.

Worse than being naïve, some of us act ignorant, which creates a hopeless situation when added with the humans unique skill of convincing ourselves of more convenient reasoning, like the idiocy in saying increasing tax on higher earning businesses and individuals is the solution to solve inequality, when there are enough taxes to achieve this if we spent the money where it was needed and it was not stolen or pumped into failed parastatals.

www.ingramcontent.com/pod-product-compliance
Lightning Source LLC
Chambersburg PA
CBHW040349220526
45473CB00009B/2822

The same illogical and convenient reasoning is happening with the issues of climate change, automation and sustainable solutions. Too many people mistakenly believe there is enough water, food, land and other resources available to sustain our children and life in general on earth. There isn't. At best, and taking major factors into consideration, we have 15 years before we reach a point of no return. If you look at the time we have left to change our ways in context of General Elections, we have only three more votes to make. Unfortunately our political party manifestos revolve around matters to redress errors of the past rather than preparing for the future.

I am an activist for change, the environment and technology. Technology is a palpable tool we can use to delivers social justice and financial freedom. Governments are chosen by you, and you must make sure their priorities are right. In South Africa, this is especially hard. When you vote, let your decision be motivated by the Future and not the Past.

What made us unstable?

Natural Disasters are a political problem and political problems are a manmade disaster. We destabilized society by digging away the ground beneath our feet to fuel our needs. Our priorities and values have been eroded by our economic system. Since the fourth industrial revolution, we have avoided all of David Attenborough's pleas, and done nothing more than paper push problems from one person's inbox to another, balancing our bloated species reputations through political and commercial PR campaigns. We can no longer escape the forces of gravity and down we fall.

Coronavirus travelled to no less than 213 counties. It has been referred to as the most significant threat to humanity since the 2nd World War and also as the Flu with the best marketing campaign. Both these opinions are right, and despite a low mortality rate compared to other viruses, it sparked a global wave of fear. No country was prepared for the ripple effects. Our social, economic and political structures forged over 300000 years were no match to a virus that is only between 20 to 400 nanometres in diameter.

Before the crisis, mechanisms did not motivate us to divide resources equally and during this pandemic people lived at extremes of their social position. Covid-19 really did not care about anyone's bank balance and global status, super powers like the USA, China, United Kingdom, Germany and France suffered as much as African countries, if not worse.

We acted too late and hit humanities iceberg, our lifeboats: governments and economy, were inadequate. Just like the engineers of Titanic, mankind believed we could not flounder. Unfortunately our digital habits left us absorbing fake news, careers marooned themselves on little islands scattered all over the world in turbulent commercial seas, leaving most without an income and the majority of the world in fright.

Our economies are designed to transfer funds and not value. Many of the very best jobs ever created are those that do nothing but move money and offer no actual service. Political leaders worldwide require popularity more than a track record of service delivery. Some governments with the greatest brand name are able to fill stadiums over election months with adoring supporters, but those same people go back to a house with no running water or jobs.

I discuss politics from time to time because they need to be taken into consideration when preparing scenarios. A *Future Thinker* will not have a preferred political party because a good democracy needs many strong ones to manage oversight. A Future Thinker can love a country but will not practice patriotism. They know we are part of a global society and the solutions to our future cannot be found in a single country's borders.

There are two major problems in South Africa found nowhere else in the world that reduce this nation's ability to deal with disasters and leave our citizens un-united, in-debt and conflicted with one another:

- People are not seen as citizens, but rather as the oppressed or the oppressor. This is determined on colour of skin and nothing to do with ethnicity or actions of the individual.
- The generation of today is required to pay the debts of the past and finance the future at the same time.

In addition to these problems bleeding hope, they create a distraction and we miss opportunities to better ourselves. I write the above with the experience under my belt of seeing another nation that went through worse than our country, had less resources, and still managed to do much better than us and in less time.

A healthy population with access to good medical care could have reduced total deaths in South Africa, but instead of focusing on our needs for the future, we used too much time squabbling over the past.

On the way down.

Looking back at our civilizations history, there can be no dispute governments, corporates and organizations have manipulated society. Some people believe Covid-19 is not a natural disaster but a manmade one developed to control humanity and its fate. If you spent some time researching this concept I have no doubt you would find enough supporting articles and dare I say evidence and motives to convince you of this theory.

A *Future Thinker* will consider any scenario and while this one is unappealing to me, I won't dismiss it. I accept a scheme of this sort is plausible and offers some beneficial outcomes. The cost would be freedom, a loss suffered only if you believed you had it to start with.

I take some solace in the fact that all of humanity so rarely comes together to agree on something, that the odds of enough people world-wide unifying to successfully implement such a prolific fate would be unlikely. In my opinion, a more likely scenario is that Covid-19 is a natural disaster which will now be used to manipulate society through policy reform.

Theories aside, Covid-19 has real physical manifestations, for example the stresses on countries medical resources. Lockdowns would demobilize entire economies. Poverty and civil unrest would soar. Our sense of power would wash away as we watched stat counters with infection and death rates increase. Those with calm minds and logical personalities would put hope in data modelling information which is at best professional guess work. The truth of the matter is absolutely no one had enough information or experience to make predictions or decisions with any level of certainty.

At a point, South Africa's decision makers were advised there would be 8 million infections and 40000 deaths by mid-August 2020. World-wide reports said at least 21 million people would need hospitalisation and between 20% and 60% of the global population would be infected. It was predicted between 14 and 42 million would succumb to the virus during the first global infection wave.

Managing the effects of Covid-19 or any international disaster needs a holistic understanding of human behaviour, viewed in a much wider social and economic context. When you do that, you can start to explain strange things like people abandoning their pets, or Queen Elizabeth coming out of her palace to do speeches again, and why we saw clothing brands such as Gap and Zara producing masks and General Motors ventilators.

I have done advance driving courses, and one of the things that made most sense to me, shared by the instructor, was when he said *"if you are going to crash, try do it slowly"*. This is what South Africa had to do, crash as slowly as possible to seem to be falling with some sort of dignity. Unfortunately when your regulations are announced as unconstitutional by a High Court, or worse yet irrational and unfair by the *Court of the People*, dignity is lost and reputational damage unavoidable.

Every government around the world would receive criticism for how they reacted to the pandemic. I believe our government had the general wellbeing of our people in mind, and I am grateful for many of the decisions made. I am not oblivious of the unadvertised reasons for a lockdown, which were to reduce alarm and lessen political fallout. It is reasonable to understand that civil unrest can be controlled with a state imposed curfew.

We cannot blame Government for our position, we can however hold them accountable for their decisions, but ultimately we remain responsible for our own state.

A constant companion during our fall was Panic, and because of its presence all context and rationale were lost. If 42 million people died, it would still mean 7.7 billion of us had to survive in a world which was shut down with no means to make an income. People allowed themselves to be distracted from the truth that peak infection and death rate were going to happen despite anything we did. Herd immunity would help during a second outbreak.

The time for our medical sector to prepare resources was needed, but an economic lockdown was not required for this and in some ways made it more challenging.

Covid-19 will not kill more people this year or the next than the diseases we have been dealing with already, yet they receive a fraction of the attention.

Even at its worse, there was always going to be more healthier and recovered people than sick.

Only two things on earth could have for certain prevented your death if you were going to suffer the worst fate of this virus: a vaccine or a cure. At least 35 companies and academic institutions were working on solutions at the time I wrote this feature with Moderna (Boston-based biotech firm) being one of the forerunners. In South Africa we advertised our first COVID-19 vaccine trial in June 2020 overseen by The University of Witswatersrand.

For some, panic evolved into fear for life and loss of income. This fear stopped more people *living* than the virus and that is why we saw some people not collecting their TB or HIV medication.

World-wide, things were done badly, for example in Tunisia, Robot cars were deployed to enforce the country's lockdown. The USA wanted to halt funds for WHO. People were treated like criminals, one report I read by Luke (pseudonym) said: *'The meals mimic prison rations, and there aren't enough for everyone', '"There are no doctors or medical staff anywhere..."* he was a passenger on a flight into Nairobi on 24 March 2020, met by their police who quarantined everyone.

Some people had their houses demolished during lockdown, like the residents of the informal settlement in Hout Bay, Cape Town. Throughout the country, people queued for grants or food parcels that never arrived. For those who attempted to keep their businesses going they had to innovate, some owners applied for support from government programmes, most met with auto responders, no reply or rejections without reason. This was the experience I had from the National SMME relief fund and the Western Cape's campaigns for the Events sector.

Many got angry, and who wouldn't when there were blatant double standards at play like businesses shut down but traffic officers with speed cameras were still being deployed.

Dispatching an army, declaring which businesses where essential, prohibiting peoples vices or stopping the purchasing items on shelves already, forcing us to carry permits, and a variety of many other decisions made had little or no benefit, were counterproductive and in many cases extremely harmful.

Savings disappeared, people developed a fear of our army and police, and after falling in love with our President, we fell out again. People came to the realization that we had to get through this on our own, that Solidarity was a fund and nothing more.

On the ground.

A wise and humble woman once said to me: *"everyone falls, what matters is how you get up again"*

The situation on the ground involved inspecting wounds and questioning the types of band aids applied. I can't recall another time in my life where I have seen so many news articles about cash flowing, for example the report from the World Bank projects totalling $1.9 billion for 25 countries, the UK government offering up to 80% of wages. The USA aid package was $2 trillion or the G20 leaders pledge of $5 trillion. In South Africa, the Reserve Bank freed up half a trillion Rand.

No matter how much is spent, it will never restore the damage done. Entire sectors like airlines need to recover from an estimated 30 billion USD in losses. Our planets billionaires combined net worth declined by $700 billion. Countless restaurants, hotels and a variety of other businesses closed their doors and filed for liquidation. An estimate of $9 trillion or around 10% of the global GDP is expected to be lost.

As unemployment increases to an estimate of nearly 100 million job losses worldwide and state debts bulge, we will be forced to accept that the greater loss of life will not come direct from someone ill with Covid-19, but from the ripple effects on our economy and our people's reduced ability to care for themselves. To save money people cancel life policies, stop going to the dentist and terminate gym contracts. Reports of babies being found abandoned in rivers and increased suicide will be an unfortunate reality.

It will get worse before it gets better, and we must be mindful of the 100 million new workers entering the African market over the next few years. The 2 billion people worldwide who had managed to climb out of poverty since the late 1990s will now have to start again. South Africa will need to grapple with around 3 million extra unemployed, a recession, increase poverty, political kick back, civil unrest, a depressed society and a fearful youth.

On the other side of the same coin, our ability to innovate during a time of crisis did not fail us. Countless businesses, governments and even people at home launched themselves online. In Tokyo a group of robots developed by *ANA Holdings* acted as avatars so students could collect their diplomas. Apollo (autonomous vehicle platform) worked with self-driving startup Neolix to deliver supplies and food to a big hospital in Beijing. In Africa, we used drones to deliver blood samples. South African comedians used streaming technology to offer comedy shows and the independent school *Curro* launched their version of online education.

Back at home, Children and Parents were reminded that family time was the raw ingredient of good memories. We learnt to appreciate teachers and grannies as heroes. Behind locked down doors a baby boom was started.

There were many examples of good will, for example, Jumeme, a mini-grid operator in Tanzania launched a Covid-19 Relief Programme, using local solar-hybrid mini-grids to provide 10 healthcare facilities in the Lake Victoria Islands with free electricity. Regular citizens used Facebook to manage fundraising campaigns and some people risked being detained by law enforcement so they could provide blankets and food to those in need. Our planet during lockdown took the opportunity to heel and the year 2020 had the greatest drop in CO_2 emissions in decades. (Unfortunately still not enough to stop global warming).

Our eyes have been opened to how vulnerable our way of life is. Coronavirus dealt a heavy blow to many people's financial positions and the ego of humanity. I am not one to dwindle on the past, I look to the Future. Factors like corruption, power shortages, unemployment, violent crime, and racism will in reality be around for the foreseeable future, and I must concede they are part of my environmental make up. What or who tripped us up is no longer a top priority, we have learnt and must not repeat our mistakes. This generation will get to decide if humanity achieves its potential or destroys its own future.

Lessons

During lockdown, some learnt how to cook and other how to be a hairdresser. The innovative started a new business, an idea which had been put on hold for so many years, now done out of necessity. Others turned into social media reporter's, or at the very least learnt how to video call. Children enjoyed crafts. Parents became educators. Some of us learnt how to *handyman*, repainting the entire home. Families and communities became stronger despite being apart.

Not all lessons were pleasant. A few became self-appointed law enforcement officials reporting their neighbours. Many finally understood the benefit of savings and the regret of not having. Some endured the experience brought on by the loss of their life's work as they closed their company doors and sent out retrenchment notices.

There were dire lessons such as learning our partner's violent character was more prominent than their nurturing one. Some learnt to let go of pride and ask for help, others learnt patience waiting for food outside a charity kitchen. There would be the lesson that comes with the pain from the loss for a loved one.

There are few teachers greater than *Mother Nature* and the majority of us will graduate from her course wiser. Despite none of us having signed up for this classed titled *Natural Disasters*, we ended up doing it anyway.

Global disasters, climate change, change in general, should all be part of our syllabus. Writing about lessons learnt while the class is still in session might appear premature, but I believe the main themes of the lessons will not deviate from the already obvious:

- Our way of life is as vulnerable to natural disasters as we are to our economy.
- We were not prepared.
- Our priorities are wrong.
- The way we live today, is not going to sustain us in the future.

Natural Disasters can happen very quickly and they will increase in frequency and severity. We must learn to live with them and work in spite of their presence. There are nearly 8 billion humans alive today and depending on whose information you use, earth can at a push manage another 1 billion people. About 130 million people are born each year, therefore we have around 70 years or so before there is a war for resources on earth. Our children and children's children will live through this. Remember, 70 years is just one person's life time and that's the timeframe we have left to change our ways.

While some are still in denial, our physical selves have been elbowed into the changing new world by Coronavirus. Unfortunately our minds have not, and it is in our heads that the real struggle needs to be fought.

People have and will always want love, independence, a sense of worth and a way to contribute and leave a legacy. Raising a family or running a business in the Future World will not resemble what we are used to. The older generation will offer little support to build a future they won't get to enjoy and the youth will be resilient to change because it threatens the aspirations and dreams we all have today.

> Why should anyone change today if there is no real evidence of a better option tomorrow?

The truth is, the dreams we had for our lives will probably not work in the Future World, regardless of what we do. Many of us will work in a business not invented yet and live in a house with gadgets we cannot imagine, and at dinner time eat food grown by a scientist and not a farmer.

This does not mean we cannot dream, we must dream harder.

Everyone alive over the next two decades will be the architects of the Future World, regardless of age, ethnicity, gender or financial status. I am confident it is possible to create new dreams which exceed our wildest imaginations. Our potential as a species has not been reached, there is still much more to learn, experience and achieve ahead of us than behind us.

The uncertainty of the Future World.

Predicting the next 100 years of our future is not that difficult to do. We have more information than ever before. A person presented with the task to make predictions on what they believe will be around in the next few years will make several correct guesses. The future might have many new gadgets we cannot fathom yet, but our needs like electricity, education, water, food, living space and so forth will still be prevalent. This means if someone predicts cars will be needed in 100 years, they guessed the incorrect tool, but are correct on the need for travel.

Predicting the tools and the environment (economic, social and physical) for the Future World requires someone dynamic, more than an expert on just one subject. You need someone who knows a little bit about a lot of things, someone who has studied the exchanges between people, technology, business, society and the environment at a macro level. A person with a history in trade, leadership and has a knack for sorting information into scenarios of probability. This type of person can be defined as a *Change Expert*.

I have come to the most important part of this feature, plotting out what the Future World might be. I have included five summary scenarios of probability and they share a few things in common such as a state of flux, tax revenue bullies and poorer citizens. I can unpack these scenarios in more detail in a business consult.

The first one is called *"Back to the Normal"* and in this scenario the world returns back to business as normal, less wealthy and healthy, but life will in a few months' time resemble the start of 2018 for the majority of us. The probability for this scenario is extremely low because of all the lessons we have learnt and a drop in support for Government.

The next scenario is called *"Reset and Rollback"*. This is where the world reboots and rolls back to its previous drivers. For those of you who don't speak *Computer Geek*, what this means is we can expect the super powers to weaken and our broken global economy degrade the fundamental foundation of the old world to a point that those who use to hold power see it shift away from them. We might see India fill a gap here. Global wealth and quality of life will decline. Trade sectors and governments will reboot, policies issued by those who can shout the loudest, or to an earlier version of policy the world once had. At its worse, this could deteriorate into a barbarism state with decentralised micro governments all competing for resources. The probability of this scenario is low.

My third scenario is titled *'Limp mode'*. This again is a Computer Geek reference and not an unfortunate situation for an elderly gentlemen. In this scenario a country is unable to restart their economy and society. Business remains sluggish for an extended period of time. This scenario has a medium probability and one that can cause prolonged damage to our environment. Limp mode could regress easily into scenarios *"Back to the Normal"* or *"Reset and Rollback"* if good leadership is not forthcoming.

My fourth scenario is called the *"Future World launches"*. This is where societies pressurize governments to make reforms based on Global Future Priorities. Unfortunately this scenario is unlikely because individuals will be grappling with their own immediate concerns and unable to lobby for this change. This scenario could see egalitarian states with decentralised management, each community self-sufficient and managed, with a governance which plays a less defining local role and rather facilitates environments for global objectives to be achieved.

My final scenario is called *"Localized Reform"*. This is where government takes the opportunity to implement policies under veil of Covid-19. What these reforms will be depends entirely on the agenda of the government. This is the scenario most probable for countries with a dominant political party and a robust financial sector. Many countries will borrow money from the future to pay for the present and even past.

A hybrid of *Localized Reform* and *Limp mode* is the most probable path for South Africa. We could evolve into a *Mother State* where we see centralised care and financial aid and grants handed out, aimed at prioritising the protection of rights, but at the cost of democratic freedom and capitalism. South Africa from this state could launch eventually into the "Future World".

Each country will play out different scenarios and toggle between them. Once we are ethically and financially prepared for the Future World we will exit the state of flux. We will know we have arrived at the Future World once we are able to do more with less and what we do is of a better quality. It will be a place in time when life is not driven by a currency, but experience, value and a drive to return to nature more than we take.

Certainties of the Future World.

Earlier on I asked the question: "Why should anyone change today if there is no real evidence of a better option tomorrow?" You have to give people something to look forward to if you want their support, something tangible. In this section I discuss a few certainties of change and I hope they will inspire Future Thinkers.

Knowledge.

People don't always want to be rescued, they want to be empowered.

Technology helps us generate, retain, sort and share information. There are entire island states having to purchase land on other continents to move their people before they suffer from rising sea levels. These island dwellers did not cause global warming nor do they understand it.

Climate change, i4.0, sustainable solutions and future tech are such important factors, unfortunately most of the human race are unaware of their influence on their life. In the future 'sharing' of knowledge will improve participation in the decisions made for the well-being of the entire planet and give us all a sense of ownership and value.

Ethics & Freedom.

These have always been two squabbling siblings. A mother might not want her child to play outside because it's safer indoors, but a child needs to play outside, not being able to will deprive them of a learning experience. One could argue that is unethical. Sometimes you can be right and wrong at the same time.

Each nation has set its own moral standards, but with globalization, universal digital rights, jurisdictional challenges, *tolerance* and *choice* might become the more important older brother and sister.

In the future, Government and social groups are going to have to work together to motivate tolerance and the right of choice, nurturing an atmosphere where people can maintain their own ethics and freedoms without hampering others. Governments that do not have this attitude will always be in conflict with the majority of its citizens.

Preparation.

The way we monitor our society and environment is inadequate, as a result we are always attending to problems rather than preventing them. Technology can be deployed at scale. Data and AI are preventative tools we will use in the future, allowing us to take action in advance, allowing us to be efficient, for this reason you will see corporates spearhead many of these initiatives to increase profit and market share.

Space.

The Future World, will interestingly enough not be limited to earth. Expanding to other planets is inevitable for so many reasons like resources and knowledge. I predict humans will 'live' for periods of 3-6 months on the moon by 2035, and a few years before that, we will have our first tourists and residents on orbiting space stations.

We will finally realize we are a universal species and not one of colour, a welcomed knock to the ego of racism.

Many people believe new technology is needed to resolve the challenges associated with propulsion and artificial gravity are our main hindrance. Our main obstacles are primal, we do not know if our species can procreate in space which limits travel distance away from earth to only one lifetime and very few planets. I do believe we will find evidence of life on another planet within 30-50 years.

Business.

Some business owners will have to accept their trade of today will have no place in the Future World. Trade will not epicentre around transfer of funds. It will be a system based on value, a circular and subscription economy. Working out which part of a supply chain might become automated, or designing a disaster management plan are part of the consulting work I offer and enjoy the most. In the Future, a company will be more diversified and self-sufficient. Understanding your full supply chain and how different scenarios might affect suppliers and clients enables a business to flex during a crisis.

Banks and Money

Banks are already aware of their imminent demise. I have written a lot about digital currencies and I love the phrase 'people don't need banks to do banking anymore'. If the sector does not transform into a niche market or move to a full services solution with customized client care and consulting, they will cease to exist. Banks will move into retail and provide digital purchasing solutions of goods and services. The bank that keeps the client in the Future World will be the one that knows their client best.

Digital currencies have the potential to empower corporates and weaken governments, they will break down trade boundaries and offer the customer more power. People will use their hard earned money to shape our world with their buying force.

Travel

Travel will be less essential for work, and more for leisure. International trips will be done with similar ease to that of domestic, with new methods of check in, security and even health screening.

Travel will be less harmful for our environment and what we travel in will define our design of future smart cities, with our landscape no longer dominated by space requirements for petrol stations and road networks.

Jobs

Technology will allow for people to seek working opportunities in real time. Labour legislation, unions and markets will all change. For most super powers, a basic income will be given to every citizen. In the future people will have multiple jobs and go through several careers in a lifetime. Working from home will be the norm for most. We will work less hours and days. The types of jobs we do will be specialized and focus on things computers can't do. Unfortunately, there will be mass job losses while we transition and the only way to mitigate this loss will be to reskill the current work force.

Most of our children will start their own business online or end up working at a business not yet imagined.

Food security.

Smart Farming will be one of our greatest future solutions. Food will be grown near to and even within our cities. We will be able to store food for much longer periods of time. Many cities will be self-sufficient with no need to import goods. People will eat healthy meals, produced with less land, water and resources. Using AI and predictive algorithms we can produce what is needed only. If you think this is not possible, *Pizza Hut* in the states is already doing this.

Medical

A healthier nation is a more productive nation and in the future keeping citizens healthier and offering access to care will be the norm. Our immune system has never ever been given priority. Technology can supplement our body's ability to naturally fight off infections by motivating simple changes like exercise. The health sector will move from responsive care to predictive and preventative using new technology monitoring and data processing solutions, allowing us to treat more people, for less, and in some cases before they get ill.

Security and crime.

The protection of property, person and information, will continue to be a priority in the Future World. Digital security will be a substantial business sector, and must include an oversight organization managed by a civilian body. Technology will make the world safer, more accountable, and crime less profitable. Some security benefits will come at the cost of loss of privacy.

Education

During the Covid-19 outbreak, China used technology to bring lessons to over 100 million school children, and now that education is online it will never go back. In the future schools will be smaller, but have more students. Learning will start at an earlier age and continue until retirement. We will be able to customize lessons and become better students. A teacher is always going to remain a pivotal part of a learning experience, technology will make teachers out of students, everyone learning from one another around the world. Online education will be the greatest tool in unifying mankind.

Energy and Services.

Fossil fuel giants will no longer be business titans. Once the Future World has arrived, consumers will have pushed sustainable and green solutions to the forefront, and once electronic transport and alternative energy became accessible and affordable, the shift in market was unstoppable.

Today, profits and labour provide fuel giants with a bit more time, but their day is ending and they must evolve fully within the next 30 years.

Power distribution (smart grids), water, waste, communication and everything that humans need to sustain life and business will be physically integrated into smart cities. Renewable energy, recycling, hygiene, telecommunications, safety and security will become considerations in the design of offices, homes, transport, furniture and even the clothes we wear. The more efficient a city and its building are the less it will cost residents to live there. Each city will compete against the next for the attention of business and families.

Entertainment, arts and sports.

In the Future World, we will have more family and leisure time. Many pastimes will merge into new virtual reality versions of what they once were, and through technology we will experience more cultures and enjoy one another's differences. From our own couch technology will allow us to be part of a story book instead of only reading it. We will be able to meet our sports star and even pick up a virtual guitar and join a concert with our favourite band.

We will relax in more green spaces around our cities.

Law

Legal processes in the Future World will not be dominated by lawyers and courts. Many processes will be done via block chain technology or overseen by AI. There will be new laws to address problems like who to hold accountable when a robot damages property or plays a part in a crime.

Courts will employ algorithms to determine sentences and prisons will be far smaller with society focusing on rehabilitation programmes enabled through new technology solutions.

The environment.

Technology will be used to reintroduce us to nature and help rehabilitate, monitor and protect every living thing on our planet. Humans will not supersede the plans of mother earth. Using smarter technology, we will stop modifying our planet and rather harness solutions already available in nature to solve our problems.

It is imperative that we stop global warming within the next 30 years or our eco systems will not be able to adapt and it will lead to a 6th mass extinction level event.

Politics

Government Tender fraud will not be possible without an advance degree in computing.

In the Future World, being a politician will not be a well-paid job with benefits. A Digital Democracy will care for our future cities, provinces and countries, using real time and open source technology, offering transparency, using automating for functions politicians are employed to deliver on today. Parliament and cabinets will comprise of smaller groups of people and those who are employed will use technology to engage with citizens on matters of concern and performance results will be available on demand.

Media and information.

In the Future World, internet, data and information will be human rights. News and social media will not be regulated by a single government or company. People will decide if they want raw information direct from the source, or able to apply filters and allow for search engines to offer preferred results.

The business of marketing will not resemble today's industry. Push marketing and adverts will only be seen if a user agrees to it, and that will come at a trade-off cost to the Marketer.

Our digital selves.

The Future World will have two realities, online and the organic, with a physical self, and a digital character. The line between the two realities will be blurred. Human augmentation will bring devices into our bodies and our minds will be able to visit the digital universe. Humans will not be limited to physical places.

From birth, our parents will add us to the system, and later on in life we can choose to leave and live in tech reduced environments or perhaps just visit these places for a holiday. Most of us will remain connected, with all our habits, history and data recorded and shared with organizations we give permission to as a trade-off for benefits they offer. Digital citizens will be tracked and rewarded for good habits and penalized for bad.

A simple and absolute certainty.

There is a self-effacing way to improve the future for the entire planet. If our civilization reduced its overall population numbers the necessity for additional food, water, land, power and resources disappears.

In the Future World, people will be given the option to use an advance medical solution to decide when they conceive or not. Unplanned or unwanted pregnancies, or abortions, would become a thing of the past. Within one generation our population growth would stabilize, and within 3, our numbers would be reduced substantially.

A medical solution should never be forced on anyone. Ethics, freedom and choice will enter a new era of debate between world leaders, religious groups and societies as we balance the *right of life* verse *sustainable life*.

The other scenario is a Future World without us.

Jean-Pierre Murray-Kline. (www.jeanpierremurraykline.co.za)

Jean-Pierre Murray-Kline is a Digital Architect & Scenario Planner. He is an expert in Innovation, Technology Trends, IoT, Disruptive Technology, Sustainable Green Solutions, Future Proofing, Cyber Security, Web & Social Media marketing and services, as well as Virtual & Augmented reality services. He is a South African Entrepreneur, published Author and Keynote Speaker. Jean-Pierre has made millions off the Internet for his own company and his clients. Read about his services and more about him using the website menu.

Born in 1983 to a large family, raised in Cape Town, started his own company at the age of 16 and invoiced first million by age 19. Since then he has worked on countless projects covering no less than 300 types of industries in one way or another, travelled to over 40 cities world-wide, has a passion for business in Africa and is obsessed with the benefits of smart technology and the concept of a Future Thinker.

Jean-Pierre's skillset are self-taught and the majority of projects he has been involved with have dominated their respective sectors and playing fields.

His experience covers Law, Marketing, Internet of Things and Industry 4.0, Property, Alternative and Sustainable Energy, Green Solutions, Environmentalism, Events & Entertainment, Photography & Studios, Tourism, Business Management and Development, Education, App & Website Creation, Brand Building, Emerging and Trending Technology, VR, AR, and AI.

In addition, Jean-Pierre is involved with several outreach and charity projects at any given time.

Equipped with a unique style of dexterity, he understands the needs of a business in this ever changing world and craves space to share, learn and work with Future Thinkers.